1 3 MAY 2017

inspirations

PAINTING FABRIC

Over 20 decorative projects for the home

inspirations

PAINTING FABRIC

Over 20 decorative projects for the home

SUSIE STOKOE

PHOTOGRAPHY BY MICHELLE GARRETT

LORENZ BOOKS

First published in 1999 by Lorenz Books

© Anness Publishing Limited 1999

Lorenz Books is an imprint of
Anness Publishing Limited
Hermes House
88–89 Blackfriars Road
London SE1 8HA

Published in the USA by Lorenz Books, Anness Publishing Inc.,
27 West 20th Street, New York, NY 10011; (800) 354-9657

This edition distributed in Canada by Raincoast Books
8680 Cambie Street, Vancouver, British Columbia V6P 6M9

ISBN 0 7548 0186 1

A CIP catalogue record for this book is available from the British Library

Publisher: Joanna Lorenz
Editor: Margaret Malone
Designer: Bill Mason
Jacket designer: Kathy Gammon
Illustrator: Lucinda Ganderton
Photographer: Michelle Garrett
Step Photographer: Rodney Forte

Printed and bound in Hong Kong/China

1 3 5 7 9 10 8 6 4 2

MEASUREMENTS
Both imperial and metric measurements have been given in the text. Where conversions produce an awkward number,
these have been rounded for convenience, but will produce an accurate result if one system is used throughout.

CONTENTS

INTRODUCTION

DECORATING FABRICS is a simple and effective way of adding an individual touch to your home, and I hope that you will be inspired by this book to experiment with painting fabric. Even though there is a wealth of fabrics to choose from, it can be hard to find exactly the right shade or pattern that you like for the project you have in mind. In this book we show you how to add colours and patterns to a whole range of materials, from cotton and linen to delicate silks and velvet, and thus transform them into stylish accessories. You should never be stuck looking for the right piece of fabric ever again, and you will amazed at how simple and cheap it is to create your own stylish designs.

If you are new to working with fabric, paints and dyes, start with some of the smaller, easier projects. These can be very effective and beautiful, and give you the chance to easily experiment with the materials and techniques. You can begin by working on pieces which can be used to cover a frame or a book, for example, and then work up to bigger projects, such as a complete set of table linen or a shower curtain – ideas for all of which you will be able to find in this book. With the wide selection of fabrics, paints and dyes available, it couldn't be easier to achieve beautiful results in next-to-no time.

Each project is shown clearly step-by-step, so that you know what you will need and exactly what to do at each stage. Included at the rear of the book is a section on basic techniques and materials, plus easy-to-trace templates of the designs used. Every medium is covered, from simply painting on fabric to stencilling, dip- and tie-dying and block printing.

Deborah Barker

6

MEXICAN PRINTED PLACE MATS

Make a set of six lino (linoleum) printed place mats using a bold ethnic Mexican-style motif, interwoven with glossy satin ribbons in a contrasting colour. Choose a fabric with a slightly open weave to make the drawn threadwork easier.

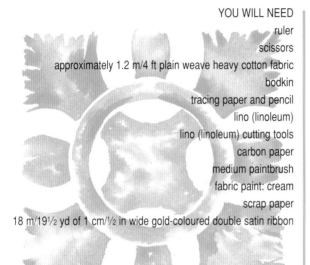

YOU WILL NEED
ruler
scissors
approximately 1.2 m/4 ft plain weave heavy cotton fabric
bodkin
tracing paper and pencil
lino (linoleum)
lino (linoleum) cutting tools
carbon paper
medium paintbrush
fabric paint: cream
scrap paper
18 m/19½ yd of 1 cm/½ in wide gold-coloured double satin ribbon

1 Cut the fabric along the weave into six rectangles each measuring 51 x 35 cm/20 x 14 in. Pull out the threads along all four edges to form a fringe about 1.5 cm/⅗ in deep.

2 Using a bodkin, draw out a 1.5 cm/⅗ in wide section of vertical threads about 2.5 cm/1 in from both short sides. Draw out 2 more sections from the centre of the mat about 13 cm/5 in apart.

3 Following the same measurements, draw out 3 sections of horizontal threads from the mat, at the top, centre and bottom. The fabric will now be separated into equal sections ready for printing.

4 Trace the Mexican motif at the back of the book. Cut a square of lino (linoleum) to the size of the motif and, using carbon paper and a pencil, transfer the design onto the lino (linoleum).

5 Using a fine V-shaped lino (linoleum) cutting tool, carefully cut along the outline of the motif. It is worth spending a little time at this stage to get a smooth and accurate outline.

6 Using a broader U-shaped blade, gouge out the excess lino (linoleum) from around the design outline. Before printing on the place mats, make a few test prints on some scrap paper.

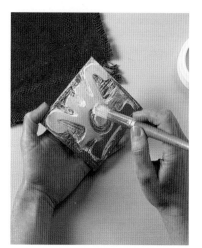

7 Once you are satisfied with the lino (linoleum) cut-out, use a medium paintbrush to apply just a small amount of fabric paint to the raised motif.

8 Firmly press the loaded stamp into position on the place mat and apply even pressure all over the surface. Remove the stamp. Repeat the process until the pattern is complete. Allow the paint to dry.

9 Using a bodkin, carefully thread lengths of satin ribbon through the drawn-thread sections. Trim the ends of each ribbon into neat fishtail points.

PATTERNED ROLLER BLIND

The effect created by lino (linoleum) makes an ideal repeat print for a ready-made roller blind.
This design is based on a Coptic pattern, using a blind measuring 86 x 200 cm (34 x 79 in).

YOU WILL NEED
ruler
scissors
10 x 12 cm/4 x 4½ in piece of lino (linoleum)
soft pencil
lino (linoleum) cutting tools
1 plain white roller blind, size suitable for your window
2.9 m/9½ ft tape measure
large plastic sheet
tablespoon
fabric paints in 2 colours
A4 (8¼ x 11½ in) sheet of plastic or polypropylene
10 cm/4 in wide rubber roller (brayer)
scrap paper

1 Make eight photocopies of the template at the back of the book to the size of the desired finished image (7.5 x 10.5 cm/3 x 4⅛ in used here). Cut them out around the outside line. Take one motif and cut out the pattern on the inside line. Place the motif on the lino (linoleum) and trace around it.

2 Using a fine V-shaped lino (linoleum) cutting blade, carefully cut along the outline of the pattern. Using a U-shaped tool, cut away the excess lino (linoleum) from around the design outline. On the reverse of the lino (linoleum), measure and mark the centre point at top and bottom.

3 Lay the blind on a flat surface. Place seven motifs across the top width of the blind. Using the pencil, mark equal distances between the centre points of the designs with small dots. Mark the same measurements 7.5 cm/3 in from the bottom edge. Measure in the same way across the entire surface of the blind.

4 Protect the work surface with a large plastic sheet. Place a loaded tablespoon of the first colour of paint onto a smaller sheet of plastic. Using a roller (brayer), work into the edge of the paint, rolling it out to cover the surface of the roller completely.

5 Roll the paint-loaded roller (brayer) backwards and forwards across the linocut (linoleum-cut) image until it is evenly covered with paint. Make some test prints on a piece of scrap paper.

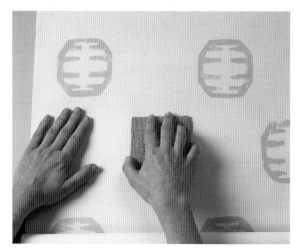

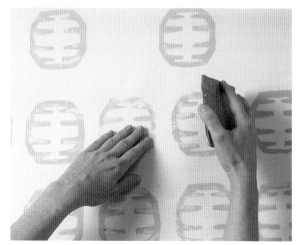

6 Begin printing the roller blind at the top from the marking closest to the edge. Apply paint to the linocut (linoleum-cut); line up the centre-point mark on the back of the lino with the pencil mark on the blind and firmly and evenly press the linocut onto the blind. Print the image in the first colour at every second marked point, down and across the blind, alternating the colour on every second row.

7 When the first colour has been printed across the whole surface of the roller blind, thoroughly wash the lino (linoleum) and clean the sheet of plastic. Using the same method, print the second colour into the remaining spaces. Allow the paint to dry thoroughly, then assemble and hang the roller blind according to the manufacturer's instructions.

LEAF PRINT TABLE RUNNER

The enjoyment of brightly coloured autumn leaves can be extended to a year-round pleasure with this table runner. The detail caught by printing with fabric paints and a rolling pin is astonishingly realistic. Finished size 45 x 130 cm/18 x 51⅕ in.

YOU WILL NEED
iron and ironing board
herringbone weave linen, off white,
trimmed to 50 x 135 cm/20 x 53 in
ruler
tailor's pencil
scissors
sewing machine
seam ripper
old newspaper
mixed sizes and types of leaves, e.g. geranium, birch, oak
fabric paint: terracotta, mustard, burnt umber
A4 (8¼ x 11½ in) sheet of plastic or polypropylene
fabric medium
7.5 cm/3 in wide roller (brayer)
scrap paper
14 cm/5½ in rolling pin
sponge

1 Using a hot iron, press a 1 cm/½ in hem on all sides of the linen. Measure 3 cm/1¼ in from each corner on the edges and mark with a tailor's pencil. Cut off these corners. Fold the fabric with right sides facing and aligning the two pressed edges. Stitch the cut corners together. Using the blunt end of a seam ripper, push the corners out and press. Stitch all the way around the edge and press.

2 Cover a work surface with old newspaper and spread out the fabric, right side facing. On a section of the fabric, arrange the leaves to be printed in a pattern that can be repeated up the length of the runner. Begin printing the leaves at the opposite end of the runner so that you can follow the pattern that you have made.

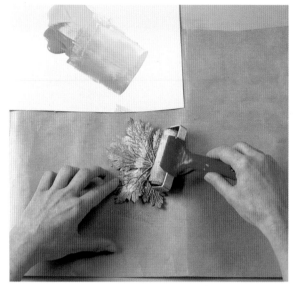

3 Pour a small amount of each colour on to separate areas of the sheet of plastic, followed by a small amount of fabric medium on top of each. Choose the first colour to work with. Roll the roller (brayer) backwards and forwards through the paint to mix in the fabric medium and to cover the roller.

4 Choose the first leaf to work with and lay it on a piece of scrap paper, top side down – the veins on the backs of the leaves are more prominent on this side. Hold the leaf by its stem and roll the paint-covered roller (brayer) over the leaf until it is fully covered with paint.

5 Press the paint-covered leaf into place on the table runner and firmly roll over it once with the small rolling pin.

6 Wipe the rolling pin clean with a damp sponge immediately after rolling.

7 Each leaf can usually be used a few times, and it is not necessary to clean the leaves inbetween colours, as the subtle blending of harmonious colours will enhance the overall effect. Continue building up the pattern, changing leaves and colours to suit your pattern. As you work, bear in mind that the paint of the previous leaf print will still be wet.

8 When the table runner is completely covered with the printed leaf pattern, leave to dry for several hours. Using a warm, dry iron, press the wrong side of the runner to help to fix (set) the paint.

DECORATED GINGHAM BED LINEN

Using a simple sponge and some paint, it is easy to liven up a child's bed linen. As an
alternative, translate a child's own drawings into sponge prints and let them have a go themselves.
This project is for one single-size flat bed sheet and one plain pillowcase.

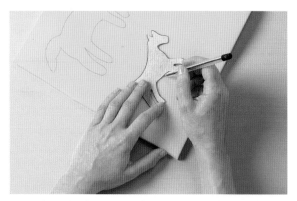

YOU WILL NEED
tracing paper and pencil
spray adhesive
24 x 24 cm/9½ x 9½ in heavy plain card (card stock)
scissors
24 x 24 x 1 cm/9½ x 9½ x ⅜ in high-density foam rubber
ball point pen
iron and ironing board
2.1 m/7 ft yellow gingham fabric
tablespoon
base medium
fabric paint: red, ultramarine, jade green, white
2 cm/¾ in paintbrush
1 fine and 1 medium paintbrush
1 flat white single-size bed sheet
1 white pillowcase
sewing kit
sewing machine

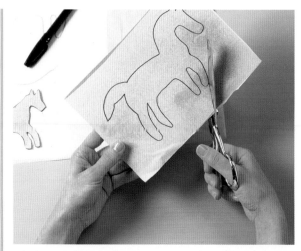

1 Trace the two horse templates from the back of
the book. Using spray adhesive, mount the
tracing paper on to a piece of heavy, plain card
(cardboard). Allow the adhesive to dry and cut out.

2 Place the horse templates on to the foam rubber
and trace around each with a ball point pen.

3 Cut out the two horse shapes. Iron the gingham.
Cut strips of 21 cm/8½ in height by the sheet
width plus 3 cm/1¼ in at each end for turnings. For
the pillowcase, cut another strip of the same height to
fit the width plus 3 cm/1¼ in at each end for turnings.

18

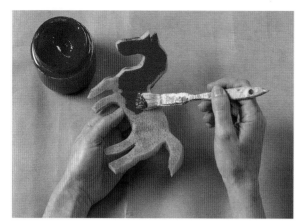

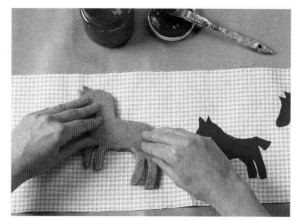

4 Prepare the paints: add a well-loaded tablespoon of base medium to the pots of red, green and blue paints. (For light blue, mix small quantities of white paint into ultramarine.) Using a 2 cm/¾ in paintbrush, apply red paint evenly on one side of the first foam horse. When it is first applied, the foam will absorb some of the paint; continue to dab it on until you can see it sitting on the surface.

5 Make test prints on a piece of scrap fabric: measure 3 cm/1¼ in from the bottom edge, and place the back hoof at this point with the front of the horse prancing up. Press the sponge firmly in place and, with clean hands, press all over the sponge taking care not to move it. Carefully lift it up. Begin to print the gingham lengths, working from one end to the other, painting the sponges for each print and alternating the large horse and the foal. Allow to dry.

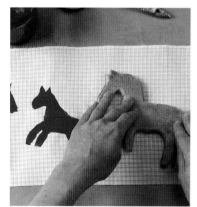

6 For the pillowcase, print the first horse and the foal, then wash the sponge thoroughly and squeeze out all the water. Apply red paint to the other side of the sponge and print so that the last horse faces the horse and foal. Allow to dry.

7 Using a fine paintbrush and jade green, paint tufts of grass in short strokes inbetween each horse. Allow to dry. Using a round medium paintbrush and the mixed light blue paint, paint the hooves and manes, and add a stripe of colour to the tops of the tails.

8 Once dry, use a warm dry iron to press the printed images and fix (set) the paint. Press a 1.5 cm/⅗ in hem at the bottom edge of the printed gingham sheet strip, and a 1.5 cm/ ⅗ in hem all the way around the printed pillowcase strip. ▶

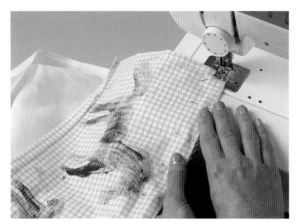

9 Working on a flat surface, lay the gingham strip with the printed side facing the wrong side of the bed sheet, and pin the edges together. Stitch 1.5 cm/ ⅗ in from the edge. Flip the printed gingham edge over to face upwards and press the top edge flat with an iron. Turn under on both sides of the gingham and press the hems. Pin the bottom and sides of the gingham into position on the top of the sheet.

10 Topstitch the printed gingham along the top, bottom and sides. Place the printed gingham strip for the pillowcase on the open edge, face up. Pin all around the edges, matching hems with the existing hems and seams. Topstitch in place, keeping the stitching close to the hemmed edges so that it does not interfere with placing the pillow into the casing.

PRINTED DIRECTOR'S CHAIR

Transform a plain canvas director's chair into a stunning piece of furniture for your bathroom, garden or conservatory with the simple technique of sponge printing. Make sure that the canvas back and seat are easily removable from the chair you select.

YOU WILL NEED
red director's chair
nylon massage puff
fabric paint: pink, orange, blue
ruler
tailor's chalk
marker pen
sponge pan-cleaner with scouring surface
scissors (optional)
Mylar film
craft knife

1 Remove the canvas seat and back from the chair. Using a nylon massage puff, apply pink fabric paint to the fabric pieces to break up the solidity of the colour. Allow to dry.

2 Using a ruler, determine the centre of the seat and back pieces and mark with tailor's chalk.

3 With a marker pen, draw a horizontal and a vertical line across the sponge pan-cleaner to divide it into four equal sections. Draw from the mid-points on each side to make a diamond shape.

4 Cut the corners off the sponge pan-cleaner using either scissors or a craft knife, to make the diamond shape. Dab the sponge pan-cleaner into orange paint, scourer side down, so that it is evenly covered with paint.

5 Print the first row of diamonds in the centre of each fabric piece. Match the horizontal line on the sponge with the chalked lines on the fabric to ensure a straight row of diamonds.

6 Continue to print orange diamonds across the fabric, aligning the points carefully, until the entire surface of the canvas has been decorated.

7 Using a marker pen, mark a running-stitch line on a piece of Mylar. Cut it out using a craft knife. Place the stencil over the design and use a piece of sponge to dab on blue paint. Remove the stencil, wipe away the excess paint, and repeat in the other diagonal direction, using blue or orange paint.

ELIZABETHAN PATTERN LAMPSHADE

Here, an Elizabethan border design is applied to a lampshade using a combination of sponge and stencil techniques. The pattern would also look sumptuous using a deep blue or red with gold. For a larger lampshade, enlarge the template on a photocopier.

YOU WILL NEED
tracing paper and pencil
Mylar film
craft knife
white paper
stencil brush
fabric paints: black, white, gold
cotton lampshade
small piece of sponge
masking tape
hair dryer (optional)

1 Trace the Elizabethan design template at the back of the book onto a sheet of Mylar film. Using a craft knife, carefully cut it out.

2 Lay the Mylar design on a sheet of white paper and, using a stencil brush, apply undiluted paint to the paper around the acetate. Keep the brush upright and dab, rather than brush, the paint on.

3 Apply the base colours of gold and white to the lampshade using a sponge. Take up only a small amount of paint each time, so that the texture of the sponge is transferred to the shade. Allow to dry.

4 Using strips of masking tape, attach the Mylar stencil to the lampshade. Use small curls of tape on the underside of the stencil to attach parts that do not lay flat.

5 Using the stencil brush, apply small amounts of black paint to the lampshade, gradually building up the density of colour. Carefully remove the stencil and allow the paint to dry. To speed up the drying process, use a hair dryer.

6 Tape the stencil to the next position and apply paint as before until the whole lampshade has been patterned. Allow to dry.

7 Re-tape the stencil to the lampshade, taking care to position the stencil over the previous work. Use a small piece of sponge to apply gold highlights.

MOSAIC-STENCILLED TABLECLOTH

Create a mosaic-effect border with a Moroccan flavour for a kitchen tablecloth using one simple stencil and a subtle blue and aqua colour combination. Hem with smart mitred corners, or if you prefer, press the edges of the tablecloth with an iron and stitch them with a sewing machine.

YOU WILL NEED
large piece of cream-coloured cotton fabric to fit your table
sewing kit
sewing machine
tracing paper and pencil
Mylar film
masking tape
craft knife
cutting mat
stencil brushes
fabric paints: dark blue, light blue, light aqua

1 Press a 2.5 cm/1 in wide double hem along all four edges of the fabric square. Open out the fold at each corner and cut diagonally across using sharp scissors to reduce the bulk at the corners.

2 At each corner in turn, refold the complete hem on one edge. Fold the corner of the other edge in at right angles to meet the inside crease.

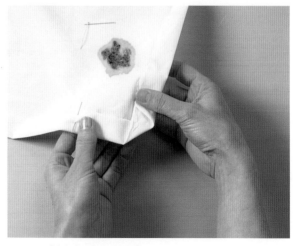

3 Refold the hem to form a neat mitre.

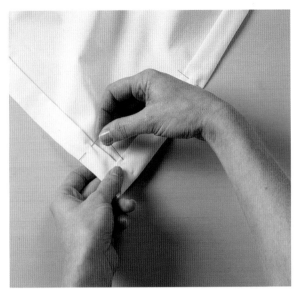

4 Pin the mitred corner in place and repeat with the other three corners. Stitch the hem close to the inside folded edge.

5 Using tracing paper and a pencil, trace the template at the back of the book. Lay the tracing on a cutting mat with a piece of Mylar film on top and secure with strips of masking tape. Using a craft knife, cut out the pattern.

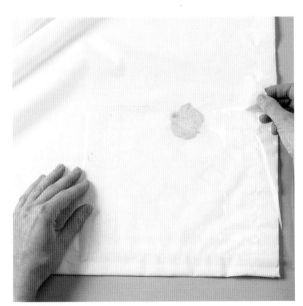

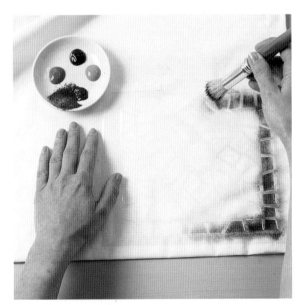

6 Place the stencil in position on the edge of the tablecloth and secure with small strips of masking tape.

7 Using a stencil brush, take up a small amount of dark blue paint and carefully apply to the outer border of the stencil.

8 Apply lighter blue paint to the inner sections, leaving the central motif clear.

9 Apply light aqua paint to the central star motif. Remove the stencil and place it in the next position along the edge of the tablecloth. Repeat the stencilling procedure until the border is complete. Stencil the central star motif randomly over the centre of the tablecloth.

GOLD LEAF PICTURE FRAME

This picture frame has been decorated using a simple square stencil, which has been embellished with gold leaf. Applying leaf metals is a technique that should not be rushed.

YOU WILL NEED
cutting mat and craft knife
heavy card (card stock)
ruler and set square
scissors
canvas, linen or heavy silk
spray adhesive
soft pencil
double-sided tape
needle and thread
masking tape
stencil card (card stock) or Mylar film
fabric paint: deep red
stencil brush or sponge
gold leaf
size (adhesive for gold leaf)
soft brush
PVA (white) glue and brush
clear varnish or lacquer

1 Cut two pieces of card (card stock) to the size that you wish your frame to be. Cut a central window in one piece. The frame illustrated has a total area of 21 x 21 cm/8½ x 8½ in with a central window of 9 x 9 cm/3½ x 3½ in.

2 Cut a piece of canvas, linen or heavy silk 2 cm/ ¾ in larger all round than the frame.

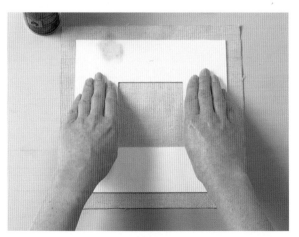

3 Apply spray adhesive to the frame and place it in the centre of the fabric, wrong side up. Rub your hand over the card (card stock) to form a secure bond.

4 Using a vanishing fabric pen or pencil, draw two diagonals across the window. Measure and cut out a 5 cm/2 in square in the centre of the frame.

5 Apply strips of double-sided tape all round the reverse edges of the frame. Pull the extra fabric back and stick it to the tape. Cut a mitre in each corner and hand-sew in place.

6 To keep the back of the frame neat, apply masking tape over the raw edges of the fabric.

7 Using a craft knife, cut a piece of stencil card (card stock) or Mylar film to a rectangle the same size as one side of the frame, corner to corner (21 x 6 cm/8½ x 2½ in for the frame illustrated). Mark out equally spaced squares along the length (4 cm/1½ in squares with a 1 cm/½ in division), and cut out.

8 Using masking tape, fix (tape) the stencil to one side of the front of the frame. Fill in the squares with colour using a stencil brush or sponge and allow to dry. Remove the stencil and fix (tape) it to the next side, matching the corner squares, and continue until all four sides have been coloured.

9 Carefully following the manufacturer's instructions, apply a small gold leaf square inside the stencilled one. Usually, this involves applying a size (adhesive) and leaving for 15 minutes before applying the gold leaf with a soft brush. Leave for about two hours to set, buff up the gold leaf, and then remove the unstuck pieces of gold.

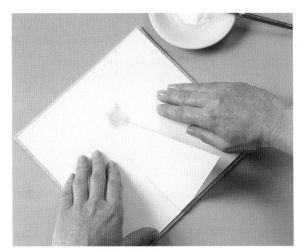

10 Using heavy card (card stock) and a craft knife, cut out a right-angled triangle of the same height as the frame and 10 cm/4 in wide. Score along the longest side 1 cm/½ in from the edge and use PVA (white) glue to stick it to the backing board cut out in step 1.

11 Apply PVA (white) glue to the reverse of the backing board on three sides and stick it to the frame. The top is left open to slide in a picture. To protect the gold leaf and to prevent dust from collecting on the fabric, paint the front of the frame with a clear varnish or lacquer.

SUMMER DUVET COVER

A combination of stencilling and sponging is used to decorate this ready-made duvet cover. The sponging creates a loose painterly effect and, in contrast, the stencilling is precise and sharp-edged.

YOU WILL NEED
protective absorbent cloth
pale-coloured ready-made duvet cover, pre-washed
sewing kit
iron and ironing board
tracing paper and pencil
Mylar film or stencil card (card stock)
magic marker
cutting mat and craft knife
tailor's chalk
string
fabric paints and diluent (usually water)
household sponge
stencil mount (spray adhesive)
small sponges or stencil brushes
sewing machine

1 Cover the work surface with an absorbent cloth. Protect the back of the duvet cover from paint bleeding through by unpicking the sides of the cover and opening it out into a large rectangle. Roll up the underside of the cover·and pin it so that it is out of the way. Lay out the upper side of the duvet with the area to be painted ironed flat.

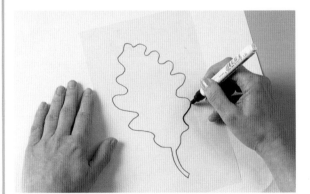

2 Trace the templates at the back of the book and enlarge them using a photocopier, to suit your design. Trace the templates on to Mylar film or stencil card (card stock) using a magic marker and cut out the stencils using a craft knife.

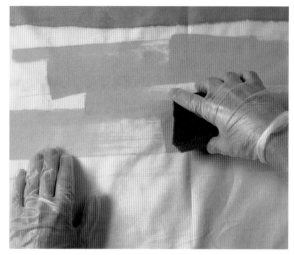

3 Now, make stripes across the duvet: using tailor's chalk, mark the position of the stripes at the edge of the duvet, making them deep enough for the stencils to fit inside. Mark on each stripe the mid-point to aid even placement of the stencils. With a piece of string stretched across the duvet and pinned at each side, rule these lines across.

4 Dilute some fabric paint to the consistency of ink and, using a sponge, fill in the stripes of colour. Choose light colours so that the stencilling will show up. Do not worry if the edges are a little rough, because this will make the final effect look more interesting. When each section of paint is dry, move on to the next; do not move the fabric while it is wet, as this may cause smudging.

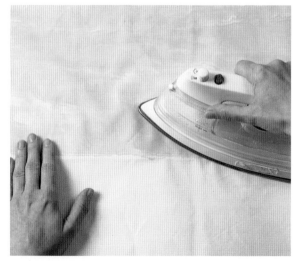

5 When the whole area is painted and completely dry, set the paints according to the manufacturer's instructions. Usually, this involves ironing on the reverse side.

6 Spray the reverse of a stencil with stencil mount (spray adhesive). Place it on the mid-point of a stripe and apply colours using a small sponge or stencil brush.

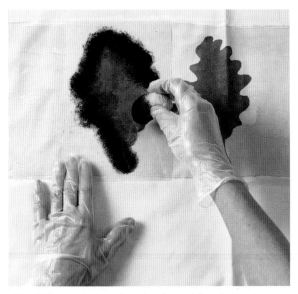

7 Continue to stencil, keeping the motifs evenly spaced. After removing the stencil from the fabric, wipe away the excess paint each time to keep the colours clean.

8 When painting the stencil, try blending colours to give the finished stencil a textured look.

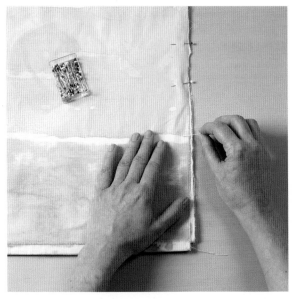

9 When the stencilling has been completed and the paint is thoroughly dry, set the paints according to the manufacturer's instructions, e.g. by ironing the reverse side.

10 Pin and stitch the side seams to remake the duvet cover. The fabric may seem stiff, but washing the cover should ease this. Follow the paint manufacturer's suggestions for washing temperatures.

STENCILLED SHOWER CURTAIN

In this project, a woven shower curtain is decorated with car-spray paints. The texture of the weave is essential for the paint to adhere to the fabric surface. The clear type of plastic sheeting often used for shower curtains is not suitable for this technique.

YOU WILL NEED
tracing paper and pencil
magic marker
Mylar film or stencil card (card stock)
cutting mat and craft knife
woven polyester/cotton shower curtain
stencil mount (spray adhesive)
scrap paper
selection of car-spray paints
protective face mask
sponge

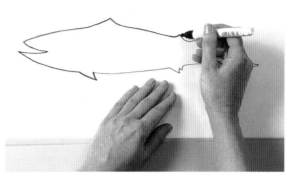

1 Each fish needs two stencils: one for the basic fish shape and one for the detail. Trace the basic shape from the template at the back of the book and enlarge it using a photocopier. Using a magic marker, trace the shapes on to Mylar film or stencil card (card stock) and cut them out using a craft knife.

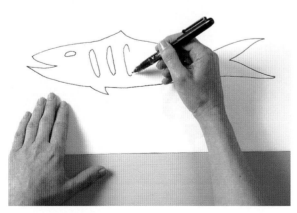

2 Similarly, transfer the fish details. Alternatively, draw details of your own.

3 Using the craft knife, cut out the details within the outline. Do not cut away too much from the stencil or it will fall apart. If necessary, do a third and fourth stencil.

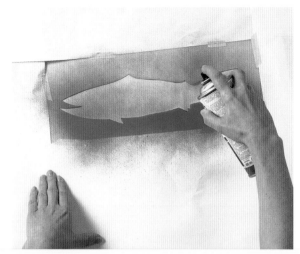

4 Protect the work surface and lay the shower curtain flat with the outside face up. Take the basic fish shape stencil and attach it to the curtain using stencil mount (spray adhesive).

5 Tape scrap paper around the stencil to protect the rest of the curtain. Using car-spray paints, start to fill in the cut-out areas of the stencil. Always wear a protective mask and work in a well ventilated area when using spray paints, as they are highly toxic.

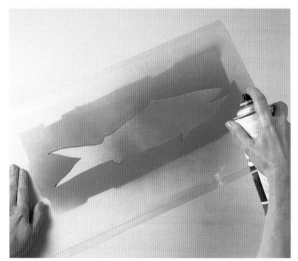

6 Lovely subtle blends of colour can be achieved by using spray paints and it is worth experimenting first on scrap paper to find pleasing colour blends.

7 Continue to decorate the curtain, placing the fish randomly. Avoid the very bottom of the curtain as this area will get wettest. For fish facing the opposite direction cut new stencils. Instead of redrawing the design, stencil the fish onto the Mylar film with the spray paint and cut out. Wash the curtain with a sponge, not in the washing machine.

TIE-DYED NAPKINS

This pleated method of tie-dyeing creates a delicate checkered pattern and can be done either by hand or in a microwave oven for super-quick results.

YOU WILL NEED
fine white cotton fabric
sewing kit
sewing machine
large bodkin or safety pin
iron and ironing board
thick string
packet of blue dye suitable for hand use
glass bowl, if using microwave method
clear film (plastic wrap), if using microwave method
bucket, if using hand method
250 g/9 oz salt, if using hand method
rubber (latex) gloves

1 Cut out six 35 cm/14 in squares and six 35 x 5 cm/14 x 2 in strips from the cotton fabric. Pin a narrow double hem on all four sides of each square.

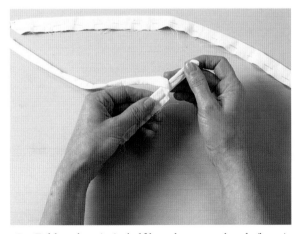

2 Fold each strip in half lengthways and tack (baste), then machine-stitch about 1 cm/½ in from the raw edge, leaving a small gap in the stitching about halfway along the length. Use a large bodkin or safety pin to turn each strip to the right side. Iron to press flat.

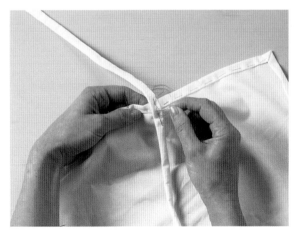

3 Locate the centre of the strip and pin it to one edge of the napkin, about halfway along. Machine-stitch the hem close to the innermost folded edge, stitching over the strip. Press the hem.

▶

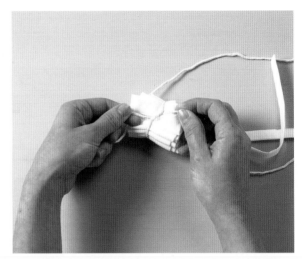

4 Fold the napkin into pleats about 4 cm/1½ in deep, then press flat using your hands.

5 Fold the pleated napkin again to form a small square parcel. Tie up the napkin parcel tightly using a length of thick string.

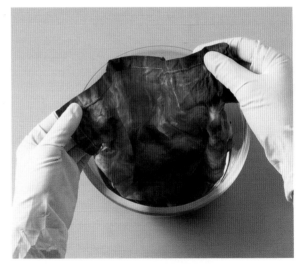

6 To microwave, place the dye into a bowl with 300 ml/½ pint/1¼ cups water and stir to dissolve, then add another 300 ml/½ pint/1¼ cups water. Place the parcels into the dye, cover the bowl with clear film (plastic wrap) and microwave for four minutes on high. For hand dyeing, place the dye into a bucket with a little warm water. Add 5 litres/11 pints/27½ cups of hottest tap water plus 250 g/9 oz salt. Stir well. Add the parcels and leave submerged for 45 minutes.

7 For either method wear rubber (latex) gloves, remove the fabric parcels and rinse to remove the excess dye. Remove the string and rinse again until the water runs clear. Iron the napkins while still wet, then tie into neat parcels.

DIP-DYED PLACE MATS

Dip-dyeing can create wonderfully subtle colours, as with this set of coordinated place mats.
Choose colours carefully, as a poor combination could result in an undesired muddy effect.

YOU WILL NEED
scissors
woven white cotton fabric
cold-water hand dye: 3–4 colours
broad dye bath
clothes pegs (pins)
mild detergent
iron and ironing board
ribbon in contrasting colour
sewing kit
embroidery thread (floss)

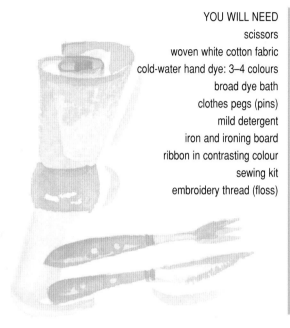

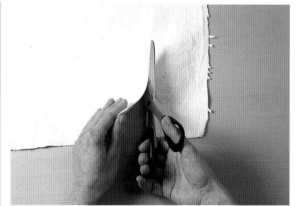

1 Cut the fabric to the desired mat size, along the grain of the fabric to ensure a square edge. The fabric may fray whilst dyeing, so allow 1-2 cm/⅜-¾ in wastage. Prepare the first dye bath following the packet instructions, using a bath that is big enough to dip the mats lengthways. Dampen the fabric with water.

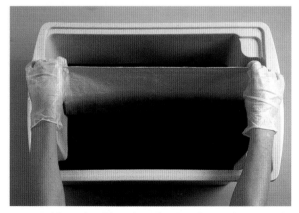

2 Holding the fabric lengthways, dip each rectangle no more than two-thirds into the bath. When the fabric is the desired colour (it becomes more intense the longer it is in the dye), remove and rinse in cold water until the water runs clear.

3 Prepare the second colour dye bath and, while the mats are still damp, dip each in the dye bath lengthways so that the undyed area is submerged.

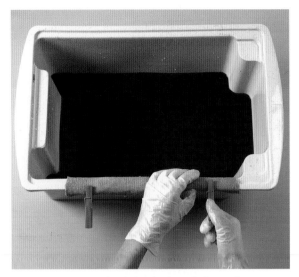

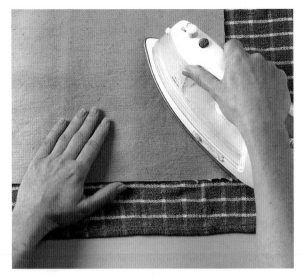

4 Prepare your third dye bath and dip each mat widthways so that half of it is submerged. This colour will cover both previously dyed colours, and subtle colour blends will be created. You may wish to clip the fabric to the edge of the bath using clothes pegs (pins) to secure the fabric.

5 Subsequent colours may be used to enhance the blends, but use no more than six on a piece of fabric this size. When the dyeing is complete, wash the place mats in warm water with a mild detergent and rinse until the water runs clear. While still damp, iron the rectangles flat.

6 Trim the edges of the fabric. Fold the ribbon in half lengthways and iron the crease. Run the ribbon round the outside of the mat so that the crease lies on the edge. Pin the ribbon as you work and then tack (baste) it in place.

7 Using embroidery thread (floss), sew blanket stitches through the edge of the ribbon so that it will be firmly held in place. Finally, remove the tacking (basting thread). Follow the dye manufacturer's suggestions for washing temperatures.

MARBLED SILK COSMETIC BAG

Marbling fabric is not as difficult as it may at first appear, and can be used to great effect on a wide range of fabrics, including silk, as shown with this pretty marbled bag.

YOU WILL NEED
1 m/1 yd silk crèpe de chine
shallow dye bath
thickening medium
marbling dyes: red, yellow, green
needle or toothpick
iron and ironing board
sewing kit
1 m/1 yd fine cotton for lining
sewing machine
ribbon or cord

1 Cut the silk into pieces 25 x 15 cm/10 x 6 in, making sure they fit in the bath. Fill the bath with 3–5 cm/1–2 in of water with thickening medium. Drop dyes on to the surface: the colours will spread out and run into each other to cover the surface.

2 Using a needle or toothpick, move the colours into swirls and spirals, taking care not to overmix the colours.

3 Lay a piece of fabric on to the surface, allowing one end to touch the surface first.

4 Peel the fabric away from the surface, rinse gently in a bowl of cold water to remove the thickening medium, and dry flat. Repeat with the other pieces of fabric. When dry, iron on the back to fix (set) the dyes.

5 Choose the best two pieces of marbled silk. Cut two pieces of lining to 25 x 15 cm/10 x 6 in to match the size of the fabric. Place the wrong sides of the fabric and lining together and pin to hold.

6 On one end of each piece, fold over 5 cm/2 in to the lining. Pin to hold. Pin and stitch the position of a channel 4 cm/1½ in from the fold. With marbled sides together, stitch the sides and bottom of the bag together, leaving the channel free. Turn right sides out and thread the ribbon or cord through the channel.

DIP-DYED CHILD'S FLOOR CUSHION

Children will love this doughnut-shaped floor cushion. Ideally, make this project during fine weather so that it can be drip-dried outside. This cushion measures 70 cm/27½ in across by 20 cm/8 in high with a 15 cm/6 in wide hole in the middle.

YOU WILL NEED

80 x 80 cm/31½ x 31½ in plain paper
18 x 18 cm/7 x 7 in corkboard
drawing pin (push pin)
ruler or tape measure
50 cm/20 in length of string
soft pencil
scissors
1 m x 152 cm/1 yd x 60 in wide white acrylic fake fur
1 m x 152 cm/1yd x 60 in wide white heavy cotton fabric
rubber (latex) gloves
cold-water dye: turquoise, Mexican red
whisk
salt for fixing (setting) dye
container for dye bath
sewing kit
sewing machine
1 large bag polystyrene (styrofoam) pellets
sewing thread to match dye shades

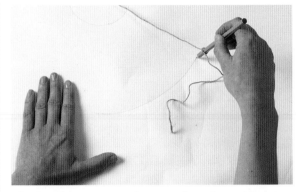

1 Lay the paper on a large work surface with the corkboard underneath, in the centre. Press the pin firmly in place through the paper and into the corkboard. Tie one end of the string to it. Measure the length to 7.5 cm/3 in and loop around a pencil. Draw a circle: this makes the inner dimension. Lengthen the loop to 35 cm/14 in and draw an outer circle. Cut out the pattern and use it to create a dough-nut shape in fur and another in cotton. Measure the two circumferences and add 10 cm/4 in to each measurement. Cut three lengths of the cotton to make the inner and outer sides, 20 cm/8 in wide.

2 Wearing rubber (latex) gloves, mix the first dye colour in a large container using a whisk, following the manufacturer's instructions. Add salt to fix the dye. On the wrong side of each cut piece of fabric mark the halfway line with a soft pencil. Wet the first piece of fabric to be dyed to within 2 cm/ ¾ in of this line. Allow the excess water to drip, and then ease the fabric into the dye bath from the outside edge leaving the dry fabric outside the pot.

3 When removing the fabric from the dye bath, take care to allow as much dye as possible to drip back into the container before hanging to drip dry. Mix the second dye colour, taking care not to splash. Leave the fabric to soak according to the dye instructions, usually up to one hour.

4 Following the same procedure as with the first colour, use the second colour for the undyed half of each piece of fabric. Leave a 2–3 cm/¾–1¼ in gap between dye colours so that the colours do not bleed into each other.

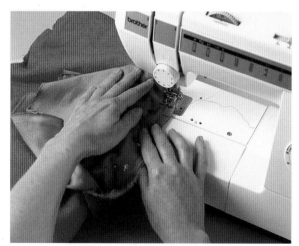

5 With right sides facing and matching pink-to-pink and blue-to-blue, pin one edge of the inside cotton circle to the inside edge of the fur circle. Stitch the ends together and the side into place. Finish the edges with a zig-zag stitch to prevent fraying.

6 With right sides facing and pink-to-blue, pin the two outer cotton sides to the fur top. Stitch the ends together and the side into place. Working with the shape inside-out, pin the cotton base to the outside bottom edge and stitch together. Finish the edges with a zig-zag stitch. Carefully turn the cushion right-side out.

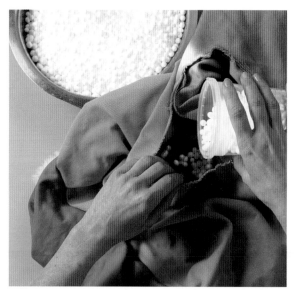

7 Fold the edges into a hem, and using a double thickness of thread, whip stitch the inside circle to the hole in the bottom of the cushion, leaving a 15 cm/6 in opening. Pour in cupfuls of polystyrene (styrofoam) pellets to fill the cushion, leaving space for the cushion to be malleable.

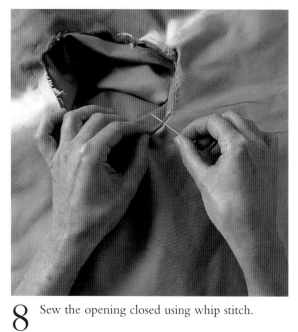

8 Sew the opening closed using whip stitch.

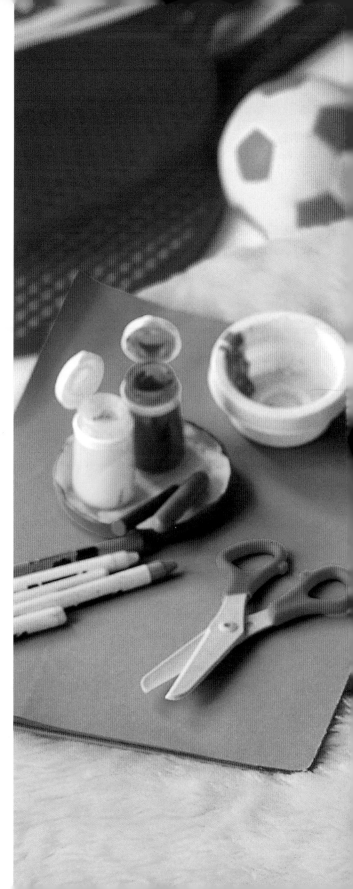

PATCHWORK CUSHION COVER

Patchwork is an excellent way to use up leftover scraps of fabric. For the cushion cover shown, quite luxurious fabrics such as viscose velvet, silk dupion and satin silk have been used. One of the charms of tie-dyeing is that it can be unpredictable and even mistakes can give beautiful effects.

YOU WILL NEED
small piece of cardboard
ruler
scissors
selection of light-coloured fabrics
vanishing marker or soft pencil
circular items for tying, e.g. coins, lentils, buttons, beads
elastic (rubber) bands
rubber (latex) gloves
cold-water hand dyes: four colours
dye bath
mild detergent
iron and ironing board
cutting mat and craft knife
stiff paper
sewing kit
padding or cushion pad

1 Decide what size the patched squares are to be. Add an extra 2 cm/¾ in all round and cut out a cardboard template to that size. Place the template on to the selected fabric and draw round it using a vanishing marker or soft pencil. Repeat the process then cut out the squares. In the centre of each square place a button or coin and bind it securely with an elastic (rubber) band. Prepare enough squares for the front and back of the cushion cover and divide into four piles, putting a mix of fabrics on each pile.

2 When selecting the fabric and dye colours, consider the effect the dye will have on the fabric base colour. Wearing rubber gloves (latex), prepare the dye bath according to the dye manufacturer's instructions and immerse the squares for the specified length of time. Rinse each square in cold water until the water runs clear. Dye the remaining squares in this way using the other colours.

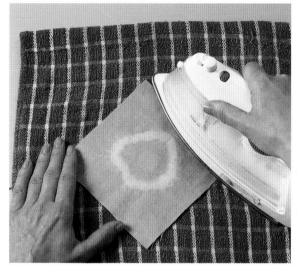

3 Remove the bindings and wash the fabric squares in warm water with a mild detergent. Iron the squares flat while still damp.

4 Trim the cardboard template by 1 cm/½ in on all four sides to half the seam allowance. Trim the fabric squares to this size. Cut away the entire seam allowance from the cardboard template and use it to cut paper templates for each fabric square.

5 Place a paper template on to the reverse of each fabric square and fold over a 1 cm/½ in seam allowance. Mitre the corners and tack (baste) around the edge of each piece, through the fabric and paper.

6 Arrange the fabric squares in a large rectangle which, when folded in half, will make up the front and back of the cushion cover. Join the squares together by placing them face to face and sewing along one edge with a simple overstitch.

7 Before removing the tacking (basting thread), sew the mitred corners into place, except those on the edge, so that the corners lay flat. Remove the tacking (basting thread) and the paper templates and press the seams flat using a damp dish towel. With the patchwork folded in half with right sides facing, stitch along two sides.

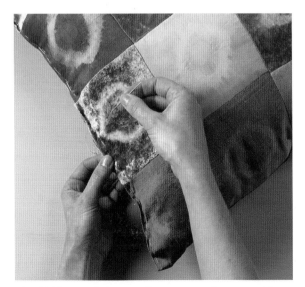

8 Fold over the seam allowance on the open side and tack (baste) into place. Pull the cover through and insert the padding. Pin and sew the open side.

MARBLED FABRIC DESK SET

Cover plain notebooks and boxes to create a coordinated desk set. The techniques shown here can be used to cover a wide range of useful boxes and desk accessories – they also make beautiful gifts. The addition of metal fittings to the boxes and books gives the set a traditional look.

YOU WILL NEED
large shallow dye bath
thickening medium
marbling paint: black, white
small pointed instrument, such as a skewer
scissors
cotton sateen fabric
double-sided tape
two short lengths of square wooden dowel
note books, shoe boxes, stiff card (cardboard) tube, note holder
strong fabric glue
metal label frames
bradawl
pop rivet tool and rivets
metal case corners
large metal washer
ribbon

1 Fill the dye bath with cold water and thickening medium to a depth of about 5 cm/2 in. Drop a small amount of black marbling paint on to the surface.

2 Drop a small amount of white marbling paint on to the surface.

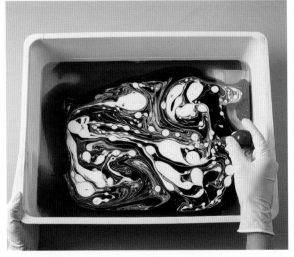

3 Using a small pointed instrument, gently mix the two colours into a swirly marbled pattern.

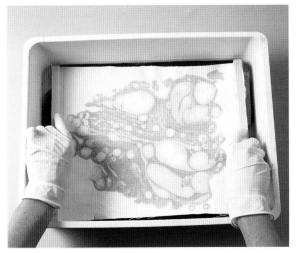

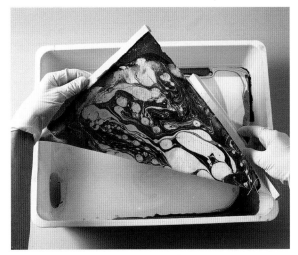

4 Cut the fabric into rectangles that will fit into the tray. Using double-sided tape, fix (tape) each end to a length of wooden dowel: this will hold the fabric flat and make it easier to handle. Holding the dowels at each end, gently lay the fabric, right side down, on to the surface of the water.

5 Lift the fabric carefully, remove the dowels and hang up to dry. Repeat the technique with the remaining fabric until you have enough to complete all the projects.

6 For the large book, apply strips of double-sided tape to the book cover. Take a piece of fabric about 5 cm/2 in larger all round than the book and wrap it around the book, pressing firmly. Snip across each corner.

7 Apply a strong fabric glue to the exposed edges of the cover and stick to the inside of the book. The snipped corners will form neat mitres.

8 Place a metal label frame on the front cover. Pierce a hole through each fixing (attachment) point using a bradawl.

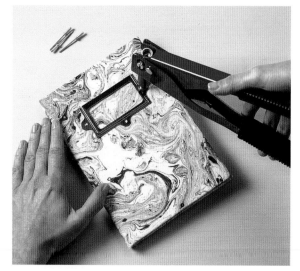

9 Use a pop rivet tool and metal rivets to fix (attach) the metal frame in place. For the storage boxes, attach the metal case corners to the shoe box in the same way.

10 For the smaller book, attach a large metal washer to the front cover using matching ribbons and attach a loop of the same ribbon to the back cover to form a fastening.

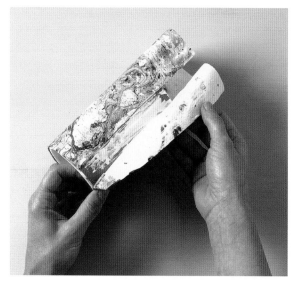

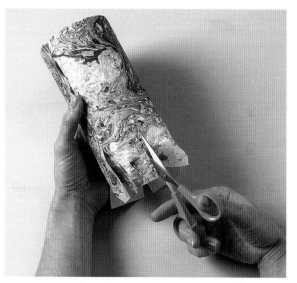

11 For the pen pot, cut a piece of fabric about 5 cm/2 in deeper than the card (cardboard) tube and 1 cm/½ in longer than the circumference. Fold and glue a small hem along the lower edge. Apply fabric glue to the tube and then wrap the hemmed fabric around it. Glue the overlap down.

12 With a pair of small scissors, snip tabs into the excess fabric at the top of the pot. Apply glue to the inside of the tube and fold the tabs neatly down over the edge and stick to the inside.

TEXTURED SOFA THROW

The large areas of colour on this sofa throw design are applied with a sponge. The detail is created by simple machine- and hand-stitching, which gives an attractive textured effect. The pattern shown is of large flowers in pots but the technique is adaptable to other designs.

YOU WILL NEED
tailor's chalk
fabric throw or tablecloth
sponge
fabric paint: dark blue, light blue, olive green, pink, red, mauve
masking tape
medium-sized paintbrush
sewing machine
sewing thread to complement the paints
embroidery thread (floss) in contrasting colours
embroidery needle

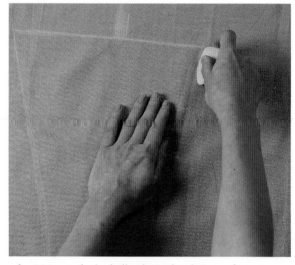

1 Using tailor's chalk, draw the design of your choice on to the fabric.

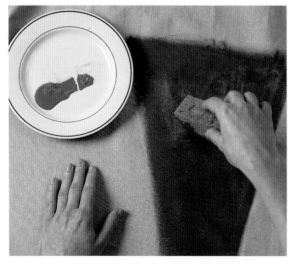

2 Using a sponge, apply dark blue fabric paint to make the flower pot.

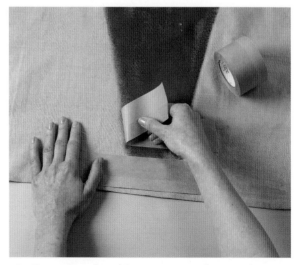

3 Lay strips of masking tape to mark out stripes on the flower pot.

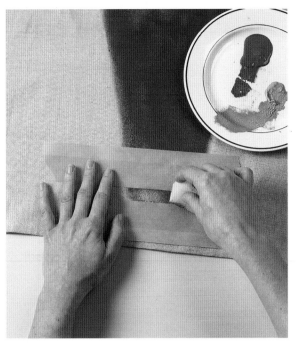

4 Using a sponge, apply light blue paint to colour the stripes.

5 Using a medium paintbrush, paint an olive green stem and some leaves.

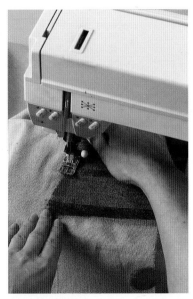

6 Paint the centre of the flower and then the petals. Allow all the paints to dry thoroughly.

7 Embellish the flower pot with machine stitching to help define its shape.

8 Stitch some detail on the stem and leaves, and around the petals.

9 Create seed heads by making French knots with embroidery thread (floss) in a contrasting colour.

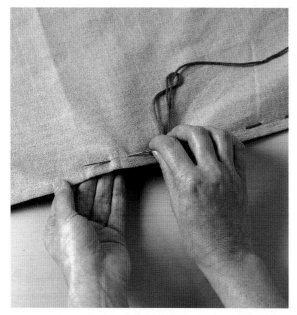

10 Finish by hand sewing a running stitch in embroidery thread (floss) just on the hemline to make a decorative border.

BEDROOM CURTAIN

This feathery curtain will give an airy feel to a bedroom in summer or, without the maribou trim, it could be adapted to a French window or garden door. Choose the colour of the fabric paint to coordinate with your décor and furnishings.

YOU WILL NEED
muslin curtain
iron and ironing board
protective paper or cloth
fine paintbrush
fabric paints: two complementary colours
feathers, e.g. pheasant
scrap paper
needle and thread (optional)
maribou feather trim (optional)

1 Press the muslin with a hot iron. Cover a work surface with a protective layer of paper or cloth, and lay the muslin flat. Using a fine paintbrush, apply fabric paint to a feather.

2 Position the painted feather on the muslin.

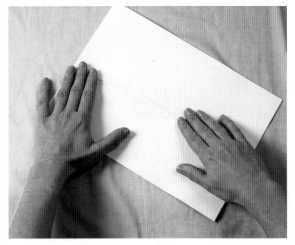

3 Place a piece of scrap paper over the feather and rub gently over it with the palm of your hand. ▶

4 Carefully remove the paper and the feather to reveal the print on the fabric.

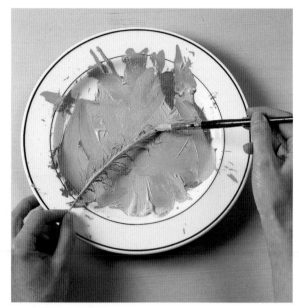

5 For an alternative effect, paint the next feather with a lighter tone of paint.

6 Position the feather partly over the base of the previously printed feather. Place a piece of scrap paper over it and rub gently as before. Remove the paper and the feather to reveal a print with a three-dimensional effect.

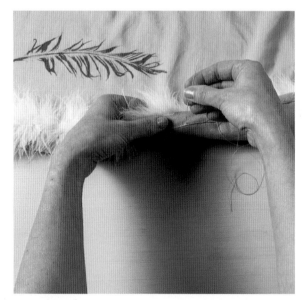

7 Decorate the hem of the curtain by sewing on a length of maribou trim.

PARISIAN LAMPSHADE

This lampshade is decorated with colourful stripes created by painting freehand and using a simple stencil. Pieces of velvet ribbon are applied to give a rich variety of textures and colours; as an alternative, try different shades and tones of one colour.

YOU WILL NEED
fabric marker pen
plain cotton lampshade
tape measure (optional)
fabric paint: various colours, including gold
paintbrush
small sponge
masking tape
velvet ribbon
scissors
fabric glue

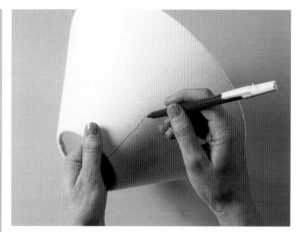

1 Use a fabric marker pen to mark on the lampshade where the stripes are to be painted. Use a tape measure, if you wish, to help mark the lines.

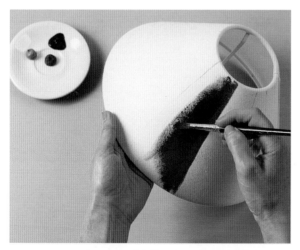

2 Using a selection of different coloured fabric paints, paint alternating stripes on to the lampshade. Allow to dry.

3 Highlight some of the stripes with gold fabric paint. Using a small sponge, dab on small amounts of the paint. Build the colour up gradually rather than loading the sponge with paint. ▶

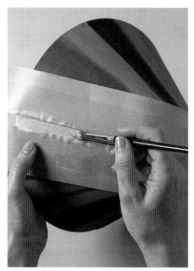

4 For more precise, fine stripes, apply masking tape to the lampshade to use as a stencil.

5 Using a paintbrush, apply fabric paint in a contrasting colour between the masking tape. Allow to dry.

6 Remove the tape carefully to reveal the stripes.

7 Once the painting is complete, cut some velvet ribbon in contrasting colours to a length slightly longer than the depth of the lampshade. Apply fabric glue and press into place.

8 Glue the ends of the ribbon to the inside at the top and bottom of the shade.

HAND-PAINTED TABLE NAPKINS

This clever cross-stitch imitation can be achieved quickly and easily with one colour
of fabric paint and a fine artist's paintbrush. To make this project even simpler
you could use ready-made napkins. Finished size: 47 x 47 cm/18½ x 18½ in.

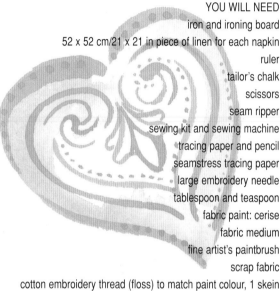

YOU WILL NEED
iron and ironing board
52 x 52 cm/21 x 21 in piece of linen for each napkin
ruler
tailor's chalk
scissors
seam ripper
sewing kit and sewing machine
tracing paper and pencil
seamstress tracing paper
large embroidery needle
tablespoon and teaspoon
fabric paint: cerise
fabric medium
fine artist's paintbrush
scrap fabric
cotton embroidery thread (floss) to match paint colour, 1 skein
for every 2 napkins

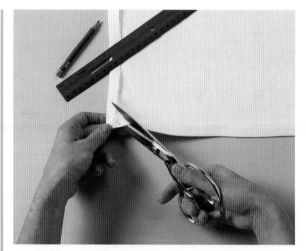

1 Using a hot iron, press a 1 cm/½ in hem on all sides of a linen square. Measure 2.5 cm/1 in from each corner along the edge and mark with tailor's chalk. Cut the corners off across the markings.

2 With right sides together and pressed edges aligned, fold the corner across the cut and sew across the cut edge. Turn the corner out and ease out the point with the blunt end of a seam ripper. Similarly treat the other three corners. On the wrong side of the napkin press all new hems that have been created by mitring the corners. Stitch the hems in place 1 cm/½ in in from pressed edge. Make as many napkins as desired.

3 Trace the heart pattern from the back of the book and, on either side of the heart, trace the required letters of the chosen monogram. Take the time, when tracing the letters and heart motifs, to get the positioning just as you would like it, as this will affect the impact of the finished design.

4 Place the tracing paper on one corner of a napkin with the pattern 2.5 cm/1 in from the edges. Pin in position. Cut a piece of seamstress tracing paper and slip it under the tracing paper, chalk-side down. Pin in position. With a large embroidery needle, prick through both layers of paper, closely making holes along the lines of the pattern to transfer the image on to the fabric.

5 Mix a loaded tablespoonful of cerise fabric paint with a teaspoonful of fabric medium. Using a fine artist's paintbrush and following the lines of the transfer, carefully paint in a series of small 'X's to give the illusion of cross-stitch.

6 Use a piece of scrap fabric to practise some 'X's and also to clean off any excess paint from the paintbrush. Complete the outline and leave to dry.

▶

7 With a length of embroidery thread (floss) split into three strands, sew a running stitch over the sewn hem on each napkin. Keep the upper side neat by hiding knots and ends on the underside.

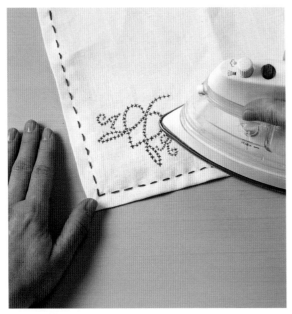

8 Using a warm dry iron, press the back of each napkin to fix (set) the paint and iron napkin flat.

HAND-PAINTED CHECK CURTAIN

This brightly coloured curtain is created using a simple technique. The chequered design is achieved by a combination of masking out the basic grid and hand-painting the colours in layers.

YOU WILL NEED

silk dupion: allow for a hem at the top, bottom and sides; for a simple gathered curtain allow 1½–2 times the width of the window
iron and ironing board
masking tape
scrap paper
fabric paints: yellow, bright pink
gum thickener or anti-spread
wooden frame
drawing pins or assa pins (push pins)
medium artist's paintbrushes
hair dryer (optional)
sewing kit
sewing machine
ribbon for curtain loops

1 Wash the silk to remove any finish which may have been applied during manufacture, and press flat with an iron. Apply masking tape to the fabric to make evenly-spaced horizontal stripes.

2 Protect the work surface with scrap paper. Mix the fabric paints with the thickener or anti-spread.

3 Stretch the fabric across a wooden frame. Hold in place using drawing pins or assa pins (push pins).

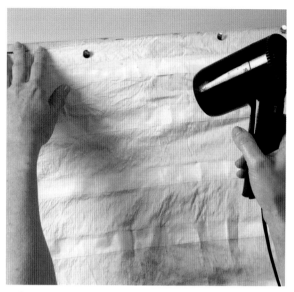

4 Using a medium artist's paintbrush, apply the thickened yellow paint to the fabric in even strokes. Do not overload the paintbrush.

5 Allow to dry. If you wish, you can speed up the process by using a hair dryer.

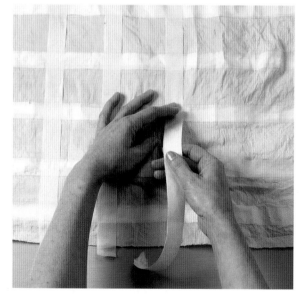

6 Apply lengths of masking tape to the fabric to make evenly-spaced squares.

7 Paint the squares using thickened paint: apply pink and orange (mix pink and yellow) to alternate squares. Allow to dry.

8 Remove the tape. The areas which were taped will have soft edges where paint has seeped through. Set the paint by prolonged ironing: use the cotton setting and a dry heat (not steam).

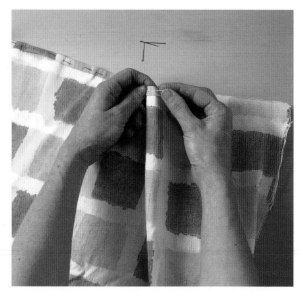

9 Wash the fabric in warm water to remove the thickener. Fold and pin a hem across the top and down the sides, then machine-stitch in place.

10 Turn the top over and press with an iron. Cut sufficient lengths of ribbon to make loops for hanging and fold each in half lengthways. Pin in place, then stitch. Turn up the bottom hem of the curtain to the required length and stitch.

MATERIALS

There are many exciting possibilities for painting fabric, but it is important to consider both the type of fabric and the means of colouring it before starting a project.

DYES

The two main dye types used in this book are fabric paints and powder dyes. Always test the dye on a sample piece of fabric before you start. For large pieces of fabric, it is best to use a machine dye rather than a dye bath, to ensure an even colour. Hot-water dyes need to be heated in a container on a cooker (stove) and may cause the fabric to shrink.

There are two types of fabric paint. One type contains binders that prevent the paint from penetrating the fabric. This gives the paint a creamy consistency, making it suitable for block printing. It can make the reverse side of the fabric untidy and may leave the material slightly stiff. It is usually heat fixed (set) by ironing.

The other type of fabric paint is transparent and is suitable for silk. A thickener or epaissant will prevent the paint from spreading once applied to the fabric, and this is used for certain techniques. An anti-fusant or anti-spread is a starch-like fluid that prevents dye from spreading, and this can be very useful when painting small details or fine lettering. Usually, this type of paint is heat or steam fixed (set), but some kinds need to be submerged in a fixative solution. If unsure, always consult the packet or the manufacturer about how a fabric paint is diluted, how it is fixed (set) and whether it is intermixable.

Powder dyes are readily available and can be used for any technique that requires a dye bath, such as batik, tie-dye and dip-dye. Some types can be used in a washing machine, which is useful when dyeing large amounts of fabric. They are available in a wide variety of colours, easy to use and readily available from most good chemists and haberdashers.

FABRICS

It is important to consider the type of fabric that you are going to use, because some types do not work well with certain dyes or techniques. Bought fabric will normally have a dressing or finish left on it from the manufacturing process. Always wash before use to allow the fabric paint or dye colour to penetrate successfully. The fabric supplier or manufacturer should give advice on washing.

For best results with home dyeing, use natural fibres. Pure synthetics such as nylon will not take up (absorb) dye. Synthetic mixes, such as viscose and rayon, can be dyed at home but the results may be pale, as with wool. Cotton is a strong durable fabric available in a large range of weights, from fine lawn to heavy-weight canvas. Easy to dye, cotton gives a good strong colour. Linen is also suitable for home dyeing and decorating techniques. It has a wonderful natural look and is available in a variety of weights, from dress weight to heavy canvas.

Silk is easy to dye, and there is a range of dyes and fabric paints developed specifically for use with silk which gives lovely translucent colours. Silk should be washed by hand with mild liquid detergents, or natural or olive oil soaps. Dry the fabric slowly by hanging it flat from a line, or roll it first in a towel to remove the excess water. Silk should be pressed on the reverse side while still damp.

MASKING TAPE

This is useful for holding fabric in place while it is being worked on, and can be easily removed. It can also be used as a stencil.

MYLAR FILM

A semi-clear plastic film used for making stencils. Specialist shops sell heat pens that are useful when cutting fine detail or curved lines.

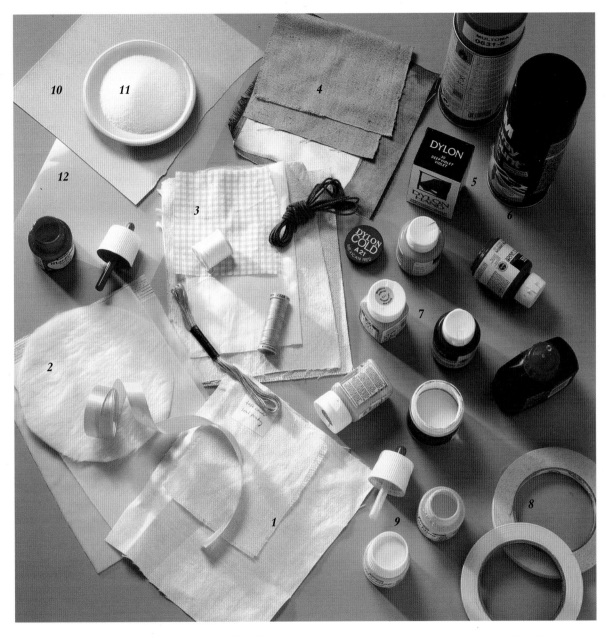

Above: linens (1); synthetic fabrics (2); cottons (3); silks (4); powder dyes (5); stencil mount (spray adhesive) (6); fabric paints (7); masking tape (8); marbling dyes (9); stencil card (card stock) (10); salt (11); Mylar film (12).

SALT

Salt is often used with cold-water and powder dyes as a mordant (to fix (set) the dye). See the packet for information.

STENCIL CARD (CARD STOCK)

This thin card has a special waxed surface that prevents the fabric paint from penetrating it. For long term use, though, use Mylar film.

STENCIL MOUNT (SPRAY ADHESIVE)

Very handy, stencil mount fixes (attaches) the stencil to the fabric ready for painting. Spray adhesive can also be used.

EQUIPMENT

Specialist tools are not required when painting fabric, only a little common sense. Take care when using sharp cutting tools and always protect your hands with gloves when using dyes.

ASSA PINS

These fine-pointed flat-headed pins with three points are easy to remove from a painting frame, ensuring that the fabric is not pulled or torn. Fine-pointed push pins or drawing pins (thumb tacks) may also be used.

BRUSHES AND PAINTING TOOLS

The choice of brush depends on the technique and medium being used. Good quality artist's paintbrushes are useful for detailed work, a stencil brush or airbrush is best for stencilling.

CRAFT KNIFE AND CUTTING MAT

A scalpel or craft knife is needed for cutting out stencils, card (cardboard) and paper. A cutting mat will protect the work surface.

DYE BATHS

Many household items are suitable containers for dyeing; for example, a plastic washing-up bowl or enamel bath (tub). For hot-water dyes, you will need an old saucepan or preserving pan. The container should be large enough so that the fabric can be moved freely about in the dye, so that it is evenly coloured. When used for marbling, the dye bath should be a minimum of 5 cm/2 in deep.

ELASTIC (RUBBER) BANDS

Elastic (rubber) bands and button-hole thread are used to bind fabric when tie-dyeing.

FABRIC PAINTING FRAMES

These frames hold the fabric above the work surface to prevent smudging, and are useful for detailed work. Adjustable frames are the most useful.

FABRIC SCISSORS

Always use scissors that are sharp; blunt scissors may cause lightweight fabrics to tear or pull.

IRON AND IRONING BOARD

A warm, dry iron is necessary for pressing printed images and fixing (setting) fabric paint.

LINO (LINOLEUM) AND LINO CUTTING TOOLS

Used for block printing, the lino (linoleum) needs to be deep so that it can be cut into. Use fine and broad lino cutting tools, as they allow you to cut intricate shapes and curves.

MEASURING JUG (CUP)

Use exact quantities of water when working with thickening agents for marbling or dye baths to ensure consistent results.

OTHER PAINTING TOOLS

Use items such as toothbrushes, toothpicks and feathers to achieve interesting and different effects.

PALLET

Egg cups or old plates make good pallets. Avoid using a plastic pallet for silk paints, as they stain heavily.

PENCIL AND TRACING PAPER

Use a soft pencil and tracing paper to transfer designs on to fabric or stencil card.

PENS

A magic marker that works on plastic is vital when drawing on Mylar film. A ballpoint pen is useful for tracing templates.

PINS

For fabric such as cotton lawn or satin, it is wise to use very fine pins to avoid distorting the fabric.

PROTECTIVE ABSORBENT CLOTH

An old sheet, towel or blanket is ideal for protecting your work surface. When block printing, it will absorb excess dye and prevent your prints from smudging.

RUBBER (LATEX) GLOVES

Protect your hands with gloves when dyeing cloth.

Above: dye bath (1); rubber (latex) gloves (2); small roller (brayer) (3); brushes (4); lino (linoleum) cutting tool (5); pins (6); coins for tie-dyeing (7); various painting tools (8); fabric scissors (9); elastic (rubber) bands (10); pallets (11); lino (linoleum) (12); string (13); set square (14); ruler (15); measuring jug (cup) (16); sponge (17).

SMALL ROLLER (BRAYER)

This is useful for applying an even layer when block painting. Practice on scrap paper to check the amount of paint needed.

SPONGES

Small natural sponges are ideal for delicate stencilling, and larger household sponges are more useful for large areas.

TAPE MEASURE, RULER AND SET SQUARE

Some patterns may require measuring tools for planning the positions of your stencils.

TECHNIQUES: BLOCK PRINTING

There are many types of block that can be used for printing, e.g. potato cuts, halved fruit, sponges, or items such as coins, where a design stands out in relief. The principle of how to print is the same as for a linocut (linoleum-cut), shown here.

1 Draw your design on paper, filling in the areas to be printed. With a pencil and tracing paper, trace the design on to a piece of lino (linoleum).

2 Using a fine tool, cut along the outline. Use larger blades to cut away the surrounding areas, leaving the design in relief.

3 Cut a piece of wood to fit the dimensions of the linocut (linoleum-cut) and, using a wood adhesive, stick the lino (linoleum) to the block. Nail a wooden cube to the block for a handle.

4 The fabric paints need to have a creamy consistency. Place a tablespoonful of paint on to a sheet of plastic. Using a roller (brayer), work into the the paint to cover the surface. Apply an even coat of paint to the block. Press it down firmly to make the print, taking care not to move the stamp. Fix (set) the paints according to the manufacturer's instructions.

5 Make test prints on plain paper or a scrap of the fabric being used before printing on the final fabric. At this stage you can experiment with the amount of paint to apply, the amount of pressure required, and also look for areas of the lino (linoleum) or other type of printing block which need to be cut away further.

STENCILLING

Although there are many stencils available from good craft or specialist suppliers, it is very easy to make your own using stencil acetate, Mylar film or stencil card (card stock). Paints for stencilling should have a creamy consistency.

1 Draw or copy the design on to a piece of paper and then, using a magic marker, trace it on to a piece of Mylar film, stencil card (card stock) or acetate.

2 Cut out the design using a craft knife. Cut more than one stencil for your design to build up patterns and colours – for example, use one stencil for the leaf shape and another for the veins.

3 Apply stencil mount (spray adhesive) to the back of the stencil to hold the stencil in place over the fabric.

4 Remove excess paint from the brush or sponge onto a piece of paper or fabric. Fill in the colour by applying the paint sparingly. Hold a stencil brush vertically and dab on paint gradually to build up colour or, if using a small sponge, apply with a light painting movement.

5 Carefully remove the stencil and leave the paint to dry. Fix (set) the fabric paint according to the manufacturer's instructions. Repeat step 3, fixing the second stencil on top of the painted area. Repeat step 4, remove the stencil and leave to dry.

TIE-DYEING

The charm of this technique is its unpredictability. A great variety of patterns can be achieved by simply folding, gathering, sewing or pinching the fabric so that these areas resist the colour when immersed in a dye bath. Experiment with scraps of fabric before embarking on a project.

1 For a circular tie-dye pattern, tie circular items (e.g. coins, lentils, marbles, or even saucers) into the fabric before dyeing. Bind tightly to make sure that no dye leaks underneath.

2 For horizontal lines, either roll or pleat the fabric like a concertina (accordion) and tightly bind it at regular intervals.

3 For lacy speckled effects, roll the fabric around a piece of string. Pull the ends of the string round to form a loop and slide the fabric away from the ends so that it makes a tightly gathered circle. Tie the string ends securely.

4 Wearing rubber (latex) gloves, to prevent staining your hands, prepare the dye bath using a hand dye and carefully follow the manufacturer's instructions. Use a container that is big enough, as the fabric must be kept moving to achieve an even colour. Immerse the fabric in the dye.

5 When the desired colour has been achieved (it will become more intense the longer the fabric is in the dye), remove the fabric and rinse in cold water until the water runs clear. Remove the bindings, wash the fabric in warm water with a mild detergent, and iron flat whilst still damp.

MARBLING

This technique is similar to marbling on paper. Lightweight and untextured fabrics, such as fine silks and lawn or lightweight cotton, are most suitable as they quickly and evenly absorb the dye. A large number of dyes intended specifically for marbling are available.

1 In a measuring jug (cup), mix the thickening medium then pour into the dye bath. Use a dye bath that is deep enough for the solution to be at least 4–5 cm/1½–2 in deep and big enough to lay the fabric flat.

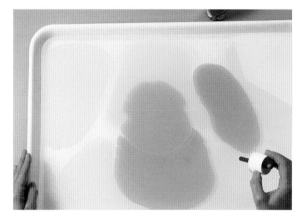

2 Using a small paintbrush or pipette (eye dropper), drop dyes onto the surface of the water: the colours will spread and float on the surface. If too much colour is used, it will sink to the bottom of the bath and dirty the solution.

3 Once the surface of the dye bath is covered in colour, gently tease the surface with a fine paintbrush or skewer. For a feathery texture, drag a comb over the surface. Less random patterns can be made with different coloured dyes dropped on top of each other, thus creating large ringed circles.

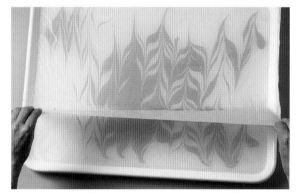

4 When a pleasing pattern has been arrived at, carefully place the fabric onto the inked surface. Place either the far edge or the centre of the fabric first to prevent air bubbles from forming. When the fabric has soaked up the dye, peel it away and rinse under cool water. Leave to dry before ironing.

PAINT EFFECTS

A great variety of effects can be achieved by painting on fabrics. Different painting tools will make a different mark, and the consistency of the paint will also vary the effect. Experiment with different tools on plain paper before starting a project.

1 Gently dab paint using a natural sponge to give a mottled effect. The amount of paint loaded on the sponge will vary the mark.

2 A household sponge is a good way of covering large areas with paint.

3 A fine artist's paintbrush is ideal for painting a precise design or for adding detail.

4 Paint applied very sparingly with a large household paintbrush makes light, open marks. When used vertically, then horizontally, a pleasing cross-hatched effect can be achieved.

5 Dip a toothbrush in paint and flick it with your thumb to make a light, speckled effect.

6 When painting on to wet fabric, the paint "bleeds" slightly as it mixes with the water to make a soft, feathery edge.

TEMPLATES

The templates shown here can be scaled up or down using a photocopier
to suit the size of your design.

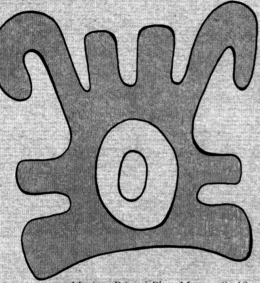

Mexican Printed Place Mats, pp8–10

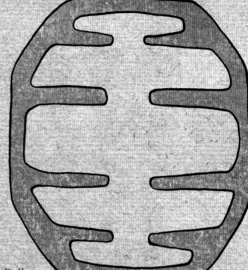

*Patterned Roller
Blind, pp11–13*

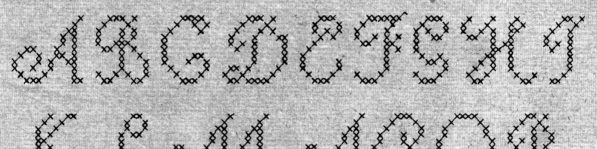

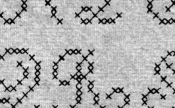

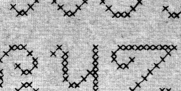

Hand-Painted Table Napkins, pp74–77

Hand-Painted Table Napkins,
pp74–77

Elizabethan Pattern Lampshade,
pp25–27

Decorated Gingham Bed Linen,
pp18–21

Stencilled Shower Curtain, pp40−42

Summer Duvet Cover, pp36−39

Mosaic Stencilled Tablecloth, pp28−31

Stencilled Shower Curtain, pp40–42

Summer Duvet Cover, pp36–39

SUPPLIERS

The materials and equipment needed for painting fabric are generally very easily obtained. Most large department stores will sell a range of fabrics, paints and dyes, though it is worth visiting specialist stores, particularly if you want advice regarding dyes and fabric combinations.

UNITED KINDOM

Grand Illusions
2–4 Crown Road
St Margarets, Twickenham
Middlesex TW1 3EE
Tel: (0181) 892 2151

Suasion Ltd
35 Riding House Street
London W1P 7PT
Tel: (0171) 580 3763

George Well & Sons Ltd
The Warehouse
20 Redding Arch Road
Redhill
Surrey RH1 1HG

London Graphic Centre
16 Shelton Street
London WC2H 9JJ
Tel: (0171) 240 0095

USA
Jerry's Artarama
P.O. Box 58638
Raleigh, NC 27658
Tel: (800) 827 8478

Sax Arts & Crafts
P.O. Box 510710
New Berlin, W1 53151
Tel: (800) 558 6696

Earth Guild
33 Haywood Street

Asheville, NC 28801
Tel: (800) 327 8448

North End Fabrics
31 Harrison Avenue
Boston, MA 02111
Tel: (617) 542 2763

P&S Fabric
355 Broadway
New York, NY 10013
Tel: (212) 226 1534

Newark Dressmaker Supply
6473 Ruch Road
P.O. Box 20730
Lehigh Valley, PA 18002
Tel: (610) 837 7500

ACKNOWLEDGEMENTS

The author and publishers would like to thank the following people for designing the projects in this book: Susie Stokoe for the Picture Frame pp32–35, Duvet Cover pp36–39, Stencilled Shower Curtain pp40–42, Dip-dyed Place Mats pp46–48, Patchwork Cushion Cover pp56–59; Petra Boase for the Director's Chair pp22–24, Sofa Throw pp64–67, Bedroom Curtain pp68–70, Parisian Lampshade pp71–73; Karin Hossack for the Patterned Roller Blind pp11–13, Leaf Print Table Runner pp14–17, Decorated Gingham Bed Linen pp18–21, Dip-dyed Child's Floor Cushion pp52–55, Hand-painted Table Napkins pp74–77; Alison Jenkins for the Mexican Printed Place Mats pp8–10, Mosaic Stencilled Tablecloth pp28–31, Tie-dyed Napkins pp43–45, Marbled Desk Set pp60–63; Sandra Partington for the Elizabethan Pattern Lampshade pp25–27, Marbled Silk Cosmetic Bag pp49–51, Hand-painted Check Curtain pp78–81.

INDEX